THE KITC

ICES
DESSERTS

THE KITCHEN LIBRARY

ICES & COLD DESSERTS

Carole Handslip

HAMLYN

CONTENTS

NOTES

Standard spoon measurements are used in all recipes
1 tablespoon = one 15 ml spoon
1 teaspoon = one 5 ml spoon
All spoon measures are level

Size 3 eggs should be used unless otherwise stated.

Ovens should be preheated to the specified temperature.

For all recipes, quantities are given in both metric and imperial measures. Follow either set but not a mixture of both, because they are not interchangeable.

This edition published 1991 by
The Hamlyn Publishing Group Limited
part of Reed International Books
Michelin House
81 Fulham Road
London SW3 6RB

ISBN 0 600 57260 9

Produced by Mandarin Offset
Printed in Hong Kong

INTRODUCTION

Cold and iced desserts range from quick and easy summer sweets to elaborate ice cream bombes and sophisticated soufflés. They need not be confined to warm weather: an iced Chocolate Bombe Noel is a delicious alternative to Christmas pudding. Indeed, a light, chilled dessert or ice cream is an excellent way of rounding off any meal.

Nothing complements an outdoor meal better than a fresh fruit dessert. Hot weather reduces appetites – and the desire to spend time in the kitchen – so keep summer desserts light and simple. Here you will find many ideas for fruit salads, whips and mousses.

Ice creams are, of course, universally popular. They are very simple to make and much more tasty than bought ones. Sorbets and water ices are particularly good after rich, heavy meals. Those made from oranges, lemons and pineapples look most attractive served in the hollowed out fruit. Most ices can be frozen in the freezing compartment of a domestic refrigerator, but use a freezer if you have one.

Most of the recipes in this book can be prepared in advance – a real advantage when entertaining. Always remember that the dessert gives you the opportunity to impress your guests more than any other course. It is worth taking the extra time to produce an attractive finish. A dessert should look as good as it tastes!

Melon with Raspberries

350 g (12 oz) raspberries
1 tablespoon icing sugar, sifted
3 tablespoons Grand Marnier
2 Charantais melons, chilled

Place the raspberries in a bowl with the icing sugar and liqueur. Mix carefully and leave to soak for 2 hours.

Cut the melons in half, scoop out and discard the seeds. Cut a thin slice from the base of each half so that they stand firmly. Spoon the raspberries into the melon halves and serve immediately.

Serves 4

Pineapple and Lychee Salad

1 large pineapple
1 × 312 g (11 oz) can lychees, drained
125 g (4 oz) strawberries, halved
2 tablespoons icing sugar, sifted
4 tablespoons kirsch
lemon balm leaves to decorate (optional)

Cut the top off the pineapple and reserve. Carefully scoop out the flesh, using a serrated grapefruit knife and a spoon. Cut the flesh into chunks and place in a bowl. Add the lychees and strawberries. Sprinkle with the icing sugar and kirsch, mix well and leave to soak for 2 hours in the refrigerator.

Spoon the fruit and juice into the pineapple shell and decorate with lemon balm if available.

Serves 6 to 8

Kissel Cup

250 g (8 oz) mixed blackcurrants and redcurrants
50 g (2 oz) caster sugar
4 tablespoons water
grated rind and juice of ½ orange
125 g (4 oz) raspberries
125 g (4 oz) strawberries, sliced
1 teaspoon arrowroot
4 tablespoons brandy
250 ml (8 fl oz) whipping cream
1 tablespoon icing sugar, sifted
redcurrants to decorate

Place the currants in a pan with the caster sugar, water and orange rind. Bring to the boil and simmer gently for 10 minutes, until softened.

Strain, reserving the syrup. Place the currants in a bowl with the raspberries and strawberries.

Return the syrup to the pan and bring to the boil. Mix the arrowroot with the orange juice and stir into the boiling syrup. Cook, stirring, until thickened and clear. Pour over the fruit with 2 tablespoons of the brandy, mix well and leave to cool.

Spoon the fruit mixture into glasses. Whip the cream with the remaining brandy and the icing sugar and spoon over the fruit mixture. Chill and decorate with redcurrants to serve.

Serves 6

Date and Apricot Salad

175 g (6 oz) dried apricots
300 ml (½ pint) water
120 ml (4 fl oz) apple juice
125 g (4 oz) fresh dates
2 bananas

Soak the apricots in the water for 2 hours, then cook gently for 10 minutes. Pour into a serving bowl with the apple juice and dates and allow to cool.

Slice the bananas into the bowl and mix well. Chill until required. Serve with cream.

Serves 4

Apricot Yogurt

300 g (10 oz) natural yogurt
juice of ½ orange
1-2 tablespoons clear honey
125 g (4 oz) dried apricots, chopped

Place the yogurt in a bowl with the orange juice, honey and apricots. Leave in the refrigerator overnight. Spoon into individual glasses and serve with Tuiles d'Oranges (see page 90).

Serves 4 to 6

Kiwi Fruit Salad

1 large Galia melon
125 g (4 oz) green grapes, skinned and pipped
3 kiwi fruit, thinly sliced
1 × 312 g (11 oz) can lychees, drained
2 apples, peeled, cored and thinly sliced
3 tablespoons kirsch
mint sprigs to decorate

Cut a thin slice from the base of the melon so that it stands firmly. Cut the top off the melon, remove the seeds and discard. Scoop out the flesh into small balls, using a melon baller or teaspoon. Reserve the shell.

Place the melon balls and remaining fruits in a bowl, sprinkle with the kirsch, cover and chill.

Place the melon shell on a serving plate. Pile the fruit into the melon and decorate with mint sprigs.

Serves 4 to 6

Summer Salad

1 pineapple
2 oranges, segmented
125 g (4 oz) strawberries, halved
125 g (4 oz) black grapes, halved and pipped
120 ml (4 fl oz) white wine
1 tablespoon clear honey
1 ripe pear
1 large banana
lemon balm leaves to decorate (optional)

Cut the pineapple in half lengthways, remove the flesh and cut into pieces, discarding the centre core; reserve the pineapple shells. Place the pineapple flesh in a bowl with the oranges, strawberries and grapes.

Mix the wine and honey together and pour over the fruit.

Core and slice the pear into the bowl; slice the banana and add to the bowl. Toss the fruit with the wine until well coated.

Turn into the pineapple shells and chill. Decorate with lemon balm if available, and serve with whipped cream.

Serves 6 to 8

Strawberry Cassis

350 g (12 oz) blackcurrants
75 g (3 oz) caster sugar
120 ml (4 fl oz) water
2 tablespoons orange flower water (optional)
500 g (1 lb) strawberries

Put the blackcurrants, sugar and water in a pan and cook gently, stirring occasionally, until soft. Sieve, pressing as much pulp through as possible. Add the orange flower water if using, and leave to cool.

Place the strawberries in individual bowls, pour over the blackcurrant sauce and chill. Serve with whipped cream.

Serves 6

Port and Cherry Compote

750 g (1½ lb) cherries, stoned
2 tablespoons redcurrant jelly
120 ml (4 fl oz) port
thinly pared rind and juice of 1 orange
2 teaspoons arrowroot

Place the cherries in a pan with the redcurrant jelly, port and orange rind. Cover and bring slowly to the boil. Stir gently and simmer for 4 to 5 minutes. Transfer the cherries to individual glass bowls with a slotted spoon. Remove the orange rind.

Blend the orange juice with the arrowroot, then add to the syrup in the pan. Bring to the boil, stirring, and simmer for 1 minute. Cool, then pour over the cherries. Serve with whipped cream.

Serves 4

Strawberries with Yogurt Snow

150 g (5.2 oz) natural yogurt
1 teaspoon lemon juice
1 tablespoon brandy
1 egg white
40 g (1½ oz) caster sugar
500 g (1 lb) strawberries

Mix the yogurt, lemon juice and brandy together. Whisk the egg white until stiff then whisk in the sugar. Fold in the yogurt mixture.

Place the strawberries in individual glass bowls. Spoon the yogurt snow over the strawberries and serve immediately.

Serves 4

Raspberry Chantilly

142 ml (5 fl oz) double cream
142 ml (5 fl oz) soured cream
1 tablespoon icing sugar, sifted
½ teaspoon vanilla essence
250 g (8 oz) raspberries

Place the two creams together in a bowl with the icing sugar and vanilla essence and whip until it forms soft peaks. Reserve 4 raspberries for decoration. Fold the rest into the cream. Spoon into individual glasses, decorate each with a raspberry and chill. Serve with Nutty Curls (see page 86).

Serves 4

Strawberry Brulée

250 g (8 oz) strawberries, halved
2 tablespoons Grand Marnier or kirsch
284 ml (½ pint) double cream, whipped
125 g (4 oz) soft brown sugar

Place the strawberries in 6 ramekins and sprinkle with the liqueur. Divide the cream between the ramekins, smoothing to the edges. Cover, seal and freeze for 30 minutes.

Sprinkle with the sugar and place under a preheated hot grill for 1 minute or until the sugar has caramelized.

Cool and chill before serving.

Serves 6

Cream Cheese Mousse with Strawberries

227 g (8 oz) curd cheese
2 egg yolks
50 g (2 oz) caster sugar
½ teaspoon vanilla essence
15 g (½ oz) gelatine, soaked in 3 tablespoons cold water
284 ml (½ pint) whipping cream, whipped
350 g (12 oz) strawberries, halved
2 tablespoons Cointreau

Place the cheese in a bowl with the egg yolks, sugar and vanilla essence and beat until smooth. Heat the gelatine gently until dissolved, then mix into the cheese mixture with the cream.

Turn into an oiled 900 ml (1½ pint) ring mould and chill until set.

Sprinkle the strawberries with the liqueur and leave to soak for 1 hour.

Turn the mousse out onto a serving plate and fill the centre with the strawberries.

Serves 6

Strawberry and Almond Shortcake

75 g (3 oz) butter
50 g (2 oz) caster sugar
75 g (3 oz) ground almonds, toasted
125 g (4 oz) plain flour
egg white for brushing
1 tablespoon chopped almonds
250 g (8 oz) strawberries, sliced
284 ml (½ pint) double cream, whipped
2 tablespoons Cointreau

Beat the butter and sugar together until light and fluffy. Stir in the almonds and flour and mix to a firm dough, using your hand. Divide in half and roll each piece into a 20 cm (8 inch) round on a baking sheet. Brush one round with egg white and sprinkle with the chopped almonds.

Bake in a preheated moderate oven, 180°C (350°F), Gas Mark 4, for 15 to 20 minutes until golden. Cut the nut-covered round into 8 sections while still warm. Cool on a wire rack.

Reserve 8 strawberry slices and a little cream. Fold the Cointreau and remaining strawberries and cream together; spread over the almond round. Arrange the triangles at an angle on top and decorate with the reserved strawberries and cream.

Serves 8

Raspberry Charlotte

350 g (12 oz) raspberries
2 eggs
1 egg yolk
75 g (3 oz) caster sugar
15 g (½ oz) gelatine, soaked in 3 tablespoons cold water
284 ml (½ pint) double cream, lightly whipped
30 Langues de Chat biscuits (see page 87)

Set aside about 8 raspberries for decoration. Purée the remainder in an electric blender or food processor then sieve to remove the pips.

Place the eggs, egg yolk and sugar in a bowl and whisk with an electric mixer until thick and mousse-like. Meanwhile, heat the gelatine gently until dissolved, then mix into the purée; cool slightly. Carefully fold the purée and two thirds of the cream into the mousse.

Stir over a bowl of iced water until beginning to set, then turn into a greased 18 cm (7 inch) loose-bottomed cake tin. Chill until set.

Turn out onto a serving dish. Spread a little of the remaining cream round the sides and press on the biscuits, overlapping slightly.

Decorate with the remaining cream and raspberries.

Serves 8

Raspberry Wine Jelly

250 g (8 oz) raspberries
3 tablespoons brandy
300 ml (½ pint) water
2 tablespoons gelatine
thinly pared rind and juice of 1 orange
50 g (2 oz) caster sugar
250 ml (8 fl oz) port
4 tablespoons whipping cream, whipped, to decorate

Reserve 6 raspberries for decoration. Divide the remainder between 6 wine glasses. Pour a little brandy into each glass and leave for 1 hour.

Pour a little of the water into a small bowl, sprinkle with the gelatine and soak for 5 minutes. Place the remaining water in a pan with the orange rind and sugar. Heat gently to dissolve the sugar then bring to the boil.

Remove from the heat, add the soaked gelatine and stir until dissolved. Add the orange juice and port and allow to cool.

Strain the wine mixture into the glasses and chill until set.

Decorate each with a rosette of cream and the remaining raspberries.

Serves 6

Summer Soufflé

250 g (8 oz) raspberries
250 g (8 oz) strawberries
4 eggs, separated
75 g (3 oz) caster sugar
15 g (½ oz) gelatine, soaked in 2 tablespoons orange juice
284 ml (½ pint) double cream, whipped
TO FINISH:
15 g (½ oz) ratafias, crushed
4 tablespoons double cream, whipped

Tie a band of double greaseproof paper around a 1 litre (1¾ pint) soufflé dish to stand 5 cm (2 inches) above the rim; oil the inside of the paper.

Reserve 8 raspberries for decoration. Work the remainder with the strawberries in an electric blender or food processor to make approximately 250 ml (8 fl oz) purée; sieve to remove pips.

Place the egg yolks and sugar in a bowl and whisk with an electric mixer until thick. Heat the gelatine gently until dissolved. Add to the fruit purée, then carefully fold into the egg mixture with the cream.

Whisk the egg whites until stiff. Fold into the mousse when it begins to set. Turn into the dish and chill in the refrigerator until set.

Remove the paper carefully and press the ratafia crumbs around the side. Decorate with piped cream and the reserved raspberries.

Serves 6 to 8

Summer Fruit Whirl

175 g (6 oz) strawberries, halved
175 g (6 oz) raspberries
1 tablespoon caster sugar
2 tablespoons brandy
8 meringue shells
284 ml (½ pint) double cream, whipped

Place the strawberries and raspberries in a bowl and sprinkle with the sugar and brandy. Leave to soak for 1 hour. Break the meringues into small pieces and fold into the cream.

Spoon one third of the fruit into 6 glasses. Cover with half the cream mixture. Repeat the layers, finishing with a layer of fruit. Serve chilled.

Serves 6

Loganberry Fool

300 g (10 oz) loganberries
75 g (3 oz) caster sugar
284 ml (½ pint) whipping cream, whipped

Set aside 6 loganberries for decoration. Place the rest in an electric blender or food processor with the sugar and work to a purée. Sieve to remove the pips.

Fold into the cream, spoon into individual glasses and chill. Decorate with a loganberry and serve with Nutty Curls (see page 86) if desired.

Serves 6

Blackcurrant Cheesecake

50 g (2 oz) margarine, melted
125 g (4 oz) digestive biscuits, crushed
25 g (1 oz) demerara sugar
300 g (10 oz) curd cheese
50 g (2 oz) caster sugar
2 eggs, separated
grated rind and juice of ½ orange
15 g (½ oz) gelatine
284 ml (½ pint) whipped cream, whipped

TOPPING:

1 × 213 g (7½ oz) can blackcurrants
2 teaspoons arrowroot
finely grated rind and juice of 1 orange

Combine the margarine, biscuit crumbs and demerara sugar. Spread the mixture over the base of an oiled 20 cm (8 inch) loose-bottomed cake tin and chill until firm.

Place the cheese in a bowl and beat in the sugar, egg yolks and orange rind. Soak the gelatine in the orange juice, then heat gently until dissolved. Stir into the cheese mixture with the cream.

Whisk the egg whites until stiff. Fold 2 tablespoons into the mixture to soften it. Fold in the remaining egg white and spread evenly over the biscuit base. Chill in the refrigerator until set.

Drain the currants. Heat the syrup in a small pan. Blend the arrowroot with the orange rind and juice, then pour on the syrup, stirring. Return to the pan and bring to the boil, stirring, until thickened. Add the currants and allow to cool.

Remove cheesecake from the tin and pour the currants over the top.

Serves 8

Individual Summer Puddings

500 g (1 lb) mixed blackberries, blackcurrants and redcurrants
75 g (3 oz) caster sugar
4 tablespoons water
125 g (4 oz) strawberries, sliced
125 g (4 oz) raspberries
16 slices white bread, crusts removed
TO DECORATE:
8 tablespoons double cream, whipped
few sprigs of redcurrants or blackcurrants (optional)

Place the blackberries and currants in a heavy pan with the sugar and water. Cook gently, stirring occasionally, for 10 minutes, until tender. Add the strawberries and raspberries and leave to cool. Strain, reserving the juice.

Cut out sixteen 7.5 cm (3 inch) circles of bread. Cut the remaining bread into 2.5 cm (1 inch) wide strips. Soak in the reserved juice.

Line the bases of 8 ramekin dishes with the circles of bread. Arrange the strips to fit around the sides. Divide the fruit between the dishes and place the remaining circles on top.

Cover each dish with greaseproof paper and stand one on top of another on 2 saucers. Place a cup containing a 250 g (8 oz) weight on a saucer on top of each pile to weigh down. Leave overnight in the refrigerator.

Turn out onto individual plates and decorate with whipped cream and currants, if desired.

Serves 8

Apple and Blackberry Fool

500 g (1 lb) cooking apples, peeled, cored and sliced
250 g (8 oz) blackberries
50 g (2 oz) soft brown sugar
284 ml (½ pint) double cream, whipped

Place the apples, blackberries and sugar in a heavy-based pan. Cover and simmer gently for 15 minutes, until soft. Allow to cool, then work in an electric blender or food processor to make a purée. Sieve to remove the pips.

Fold the cream into the purée. Spoon into individual dishes and chill. Serve with Cigarettes Russes (see page [illegible])

Serves 6

Autumn Pudding

500 g (1 lb) cooking apples, peeled, cored and sliced
375 g (12 oz) blackberries
50 g (2 oz) soft brown sugar
2 tablespoons water
3 tablespoons port
8 slices brown bread, crusts removed

Place the apples, blackberries and sugar in a heavy-based pan with the water. Cover and simmer gently until soft but not pulpy. Add the port and leave to cool. Strain, reserving the juice.

Cut 3 circles of bread to fit the base, middle and top of a 900 ml (1½ pint) pudding basin. Shape the remaining bread to fit around the side of the basin.

Soak the bread in the reserved fruit juice as you line the basin. Start with the small circle in the bottom of the basin, then the shaped bread round the side. Spoon in half the fruit and place the middle-sized circle of bread on top. Cover with the remaining fruit then top with the large bread circle. Fold over any bread protruding over the top of the basin. Cover with a saucer small enough to fit inside the basin and put a 500 g (1 lb) weight on top. Leave in the refrigerator overnight.

Turn onto a serving plate, pour over any remaining fruit juice and serve with whipped cream.

Serves 6 to 8

Cider Syllabub

284 ml (½ pint) double cream
grated rind and juice of 1 lemon
120 ml (4 fl oz) sweet cider
2 egg whites
50 g (2 oz) caster sugar

Put the cream and lemon rind in a bowl and whisk until thick. Gradually add the lemon juice and cider and continue whisking until it holds its shape.

Whisk the egg whites until stiff. Whisk in the sugar, then carefully fold in the cream mixture.

Spoon into glasses and serve with Nutty Curls (see page 86).

Serves 6

Orange Syllabub in Lace Baskets

grated rind and juice of 2 oranges
2 tablespoons Grand Marnier
284 ml (½ pint) double cream
2 egg whites
50 g (2 oz) caster sugar
8 Lace Baskets (see page 91)
finely shredded orange rind to decorate

Place the orange rind and juice in a bowl with the liqueur.

Whip the cream until it stands in peaks, then gradually add the orange mixture and continue whisking until it holds its shape.

Whisk the egg whites until stiff, then whisk in the sugar. Carefully fold into the cream mixture.

Spoon carefully into the Lace Baskets and sprinkle with orange rind.

Serves 8

Avocado and Lime Whip

2 ripe avocado pears, peeled and stoned
2 limes
6 tablespoons single cream
2 egg whites
50 g (2 oz) icing sugar, sifted

Chop the avocados and place in an electric blender or food processor. Strain the juice of 1 lime and add to the blender or processor with the cream. Work to a purée.

Whisk the egg whites until stiff, then whisk in the icing sugar, a tablespoon at a time. Carefully fold in the avocado mixture and spoon into individual glasses.

Slice half the remaining lime thinly, place a slice on each glass and spoon a little juice from the other half over each one. Serve immediately, with Cigarettes Russes (see page 88).

Serves 4

Passion Fruit and Banana Whip

3 passion fruit
2 bananas
1 tablespoon lemon juice
142 ml (5 fl oz) double cream, whipped

Cut the passion fruit in half and scoop out the pulp. Mash the bananas to a purée with the lemon juice, then mix with the passion fruit. Fold in the cream and spoon into individual serving dishes. Serve immediately, with Langues de Chat biscuits (see page 87).

Serves 4

Mango Mousse

2 mangoes
75 g (3 oz) icing sugar, sifted
juice of 1 lime or small lemon
2 teaspoons gelatine, soaked in 2 tablespoons cold water
284 ml (½ pint) double cream, whipped
lime or lemon twists to decorate

Cut the mangoes in half lengthways, scrape out the flesh and place in a blender or food processor. Add the icing sugar and lime or lemon juice and blend until smooth.

Heat the gelatine gently until dissolved. Cool slightly, then mix into the mango purée with the cream. Pour into individual glass bowls and leave to set.

Decorate with lime or lemon twists.

Serves 6

Gooseberry Mousse

500 g (1 lb) gooseberries
3 tablespoons water
175 g (6 oz) caster sugar
2 heads of elderflower, tied in muslin (optional)
2 eggs
1 egg yolk
15 g (½ oz) gelatine, soaked in 3 tablespoons cold water
142 ml (5 fl oz) whipping cream, whipped
TO DECORATE:
120 ml (4 fl oz) double cream, whipped
1 kiwi fruit, sliced

Place the gooseberries in a pan with the water, half the sugar and the elderflower, if using. Cover and cook gently for 10 to 15 minutes, until soft. Remove the elderflower and leave to cool. Purée in an electric blender or food processor, then sieve to remove the tops and tails.

Place the eggs, egg yolk and remaining sugar in a bowl and beat with an electric whisk until thick and mousse-like.

Heat the gelatine gently until dissolved. Mix into the gooseberry purée and cool slightly. Carefully fold into the egg mixture with the whipping cream. Turn into a glass bowl and chill until set.

Decorate with piped cream and kiwi fruit slices.

Serves 8

Damson Mousse

500 g (1 lb) damsons
4 tablespoons water
250 g (8 oz) caster sugar
2 eggs
1 egg yolk
15 g (½ oz) gelatine, soaked in 3 tablespoons cold water
284 ml (½ pint) whipping cream, whipped
4 tablespoons double cream, whipped, to decorate

Place the damsons in a pan with the water and half the sugar. Cover and cook gently for 15 minutes, until tender. Cool slightly, remove the stones, then purée in an electric blender or food processor. Sieve to remove the skins. Leave to cool.

Place the eggs, egg yolk and remaining sugar in a bowl and beat with an electric whisk until thick and mousse-like.

Heat the gelatine gently until dissolved. Mix into the damson purée. When it is just beginning to set, carefully fold into the egg mixture with the whipping cream.

Turn into a 1.75 litre (3 pint) ring mould and chill until set. Turn out onto a serving plate and decorate with piped cream.

Serves 8

Peach and Apricot Fool

250 g (8 oz) dried apricots, soaked overnight in 450 ml (3/4 pint) water
grated rind and juice of 1 lemon
50 g (2 oz) caster sugar
3 peaches
2 tablespoons apricot brandy
284 ml (1/2 pint) double cream, whipped

Put the apricots in a saucepan with their soaking water. Add the lemon rind and simmer for 15 to 20 minutes. Drain, reserving 6 tablespoons of the liquid. Cool the apricots and purée in an electric blender or food processor with the reserved liquid, lemon juice and sugar.

Peel and slice the peaches and place in a bowl with the apricot brandy. Stir, then leave to soak for 30 minutes. Reserve 6 peach slices for decoration.

Divide the remaining peach slices between 6 tall glasses. Fold the juice into the apricot purée with three quarters of the cream. Spoon the apricot mixture over the peaches.

Pipe the remaining cream in swirls on top of the fools and decorate with the reserved peach slices.

Serves 6

Crunchy Apple Whip

125 g (4 oz) ginger snaps, crushed
50 g (2 oz) chopped roasted hazelnuts
3 tablespoons clear honey
grated rind and juice of 1 lemon
500 g (1 lb) cooking apples, peeled, cored and sliced
1 egg white
25 g (1 oz) caster sugar
142 ml (5 fl oz) double cream, whipped

Mix together the ginger snaps and hazelnuts; set aside.

Put the honey, lemon rind and juice, and apples in a pan. Cover and simmer gently for 10 minutes until the apples are soft. Sieve and leave to cool.

Whisk the egg white until stiff, then whisk in the sugar. Fold into the apple purée with the cream. Divide half the fruit between 6 tall glasses and cover with half the biscuit mixture. Repeat these layers, finishing with a layer of biscuit mixture. Chill before serving.

Serves 6

Apricot Cream Layer

250 g (8 oz) dried apricots, chopped
300 ml (½ pint) apple juice
142 ml (5 fl oz) double cream
1 tablespoon brandy
2 teaspoons icing sugar
1 tablespoon chopped almonds, toasted

Place the apricots in a pan with the apple juice and soak for 3 hours. Add 4 tablespoons water, bring to the boil and simmer gently for 30 minutes, until the apricots are soft. Leave to cool.

Whip the cream with the brandy and icing sugar until it stands in soft peaks. Spoon half the apricot mixture into 4 glasses and cover with half the cream; repeat the layers. Sprinkle with the almonds and serve chilled.
Serves 4

Lemon and Apple Cheesecake

75 g (3 oz) margarine, melted
250 g (8 oz) ginger snaps, crushed
25 g (1 oz) demerara sugar
250 g (8 oz) cooking apples, peeled, cored and sliced
1 tablespoon water
227 g (8 oz) curd cheese
50 g (2 oz) caster sugar
grated rind and juice of 1 lemon
15 g (½ oz) gelatine, soaked in 3 tablespoons cold water
250 ml (8 fl oz) double cream, whipped
lemon twists to decorate

Combine the margarine, biscuit crumbs and demerara sugar. Press over the base and sides of a 23 cm (9 inch) flan dish. Chill until firm.

Place the apples and water in a pan, cover and simmer gently for 10 to 15 minutes. Work in an electric blender or food processor until smooth; cool.

Place the cheese in a bowl and beat in the caster sugar and lemon rind. Mix the lemon juice into the apple purée and stir into the cheese mixture. Heat the gelatine gently until dissolved then stir into the cheese mixture with two thirds of the cream.

Spoon into the crumb case, smooth the surface and leave in the refrigerator to set.

Decorate with the remaining cream and lemon twists.

Serves 6 to 8

Kiwi and Gooseberry Cheesecake

40 g (1½ oz) butter
125 g (4 oz) ginger snaps, crushed
500 g (1 lb) gooseberries
125 g (4 oz) caster sugar
2 heads of elderflower, tied in muslin (optional)
15 g (½ oz) gelatine, soaked in 3 tablespoons cold water
227 g (8 oz) curd cheese
few drops of green food colouring
142 ml (5 fl oz) double cream, whipped
3 kiwi fruit, peeled and thinly sliced

Melt the butter in a pan and stir in the biscuit crumbs. Spread the mixture over the base of a greased 18 cm (7 inch) loose-bottomed cake tin and chill until firm.

Place the gooseberries in a pan with the sugar and elderflower, if using. Cover and simmer for 10 to 15 minutes, until soft. Leave to cool, then remove the elderflower. Sieve or work in an electric blender or food processor until smooth.

Heat the gelatine gently until dissolved; stir into the gooseberry purée. Beat the cheese in a bowl to soften, then mix in the colouring, purée and cream. Turn into the tin and place in the refrigerator to set.

Remove the cheesecake from the tin and place on a serving plate. Arrange overlapping slices of kiwi fruit around the edge to serve.

Serves 6 to 8

Peach Meringue Basket

MERINGUE:
5 egg whites
325 g (11 oz) icing sugar, sifted
few drops of vanilla essence
FILLING:
284 ml (½ pint) double cream, lightly whipped
6 ripe peaches, peeled and sliced
2 tablespoons kirsch

Whisk the egg whites until stiff, then gradually whisk in the icing sugar with the vanilla. Place the bowl over a pan of simmering water and whisk for about 5 minutes, until very stiff.

Line 2 large baking sheets with silicone paper and draw four 15 cm (6 inch) circles on each. Put most of the meringue in a piping bag fitted with a large fluted nozzle. Pipe a base on one circle and a ring of meringue on the other circles.

Bake in a preheated cool oven, 150°C (300°F), Gas Mark 2, for 50 minutes. Fill the piping bag with the remaining meringue.

Remove the rings from the paper and place one on top of the other on the base, fixing them with a little uncooked meringue. Pipe vertical lines of meringue round the basket. Return to the oven for 1 hour. Cool on a wire rack; remove the paper.

Reserve 2 tablespoons cream. Fold the slices from 4 peaches into the remaining cream, with the kirsch. Spoon into the basket and top with the remaining peach slices and cream.
Serves 6 to 8

Lemon Meringues

4 egg whites
275 g (9 oz) caster sugar
113 g (4 oz) cream cheese
grated rind and juice of 1 lemon
142 ml (5 fl oz) double cream, whipped
TO DECORATE:
6 lemon twists
frosted currant leaves, page 43 (optional)

Whisk the egg whites until stiff, then whisk in half the sugar. Fold in all but 2 tablespoons of the remaining sugar.

Spoon the meringue into 12 mounds on a baking sheet lined with silicone paper. Bake in a preheated cool oven, 140°C (275°F), Gas Mark 1, for 2 hours. Peel off the paper and cool.

Beat together the cheese, reserved sugar, lemon rind and juice. Fold in the cream and use to sandwich the meringues. Decorate with lemon twists and frosted leaves, if desired.
Serves 6

Watermelon Ice

½ small watermelon, weighing about 1.25 kg (2½ lb)
125 g (4 oz) icing sugar, sifted
juice of 1 small lemon
mint sprigs to decorate

Discard the seeds and scoop out the flesh from the watermelon, reserving the shell. Cut the shell into 4 wedges. Place in a freezerproof bowl of matching size and re-shape. Chill.

Place the flesh in a blender or food processor with the sugar and lemon juice and work until smooth. Pour into a rigid freezerproof container and freeze for 3 to 4 hours. Turn into a chilled bowl and whisk until fluffy.

Turn into the melon shell and smooth the top. Cover with foil and freeze until solid.

Separate the melon wedges, using a warmed knife, 10 minutes before serving. Decorate with mint sprigs.
Serves 4

Melon Sherbet

1 melon (preferably Charentais), weighing 1 kg (2 lb)
50 g (2 oz) icing sugar
juice of 1 lime or small lemon
1 egg white

Cut the melon in half, scoop out and discard the seeds. Scoop out the flesh with a spoon and reserve the shells. Place the flesh in an electric blender or food processor with the icing sugar and lime or lemon juice. Work to a purée, then pour into a rigid freezerproof container, cover, seal and freeze for 2 to 3 hours.

Whisk to break up the ice crystals. Whisk the egg white until stiff, then whisk into the half-frozen melon mixture. Return to the freezer until firm.

Transfer to the refrigerator 20 minutes before serving to soften. Scoop into the melon shells.

Serves 4 to 6

Elderflower Sorbet

A delicious sorbet to make in the short elderflower season.

450 ml (¾ pint) water
125 g (4 oz) caster sugar
thinly pared rind and juice of 2 lemons
25 g (1 oz) elderflower heads
1 egg white
elderflower or mint leaves to decorate

Put the water, sugar and lemon rind in a pan and heat gently, stirring until the sugar has dissolved. Bring to the boil, then simmer for 5 minutes. Add the elderflower and lemon juice, cover and leave to cool.

Strain into a rigid freezerproof container, cover, seal and freeze for 2 to 3 hours, until half frozen.

Whisk the egg white until stiff, then whisk into the ice. Cover, seal and freeze until firm.

Transfer to the refrigerator 10 minutes before serving to soften. Scoop into chilled glasses and top with elderflower or mint leaves.

Serves 6

Thyme and Honey Sorbet

4 large lemons
600 ml (1 pint) water
75 g (3 oz) caster sugar
large bunch of thyme
3 tablespoons clear honey
1 egg white
4 thyme sprigs to decorate

Cut a thin slice from the base of each lemon so that they will stand. Cut the tops off the lemons and carefully scrape out the flesh. Sieve to extract the juice. Reserve the shells.

Put the water, sugar and thyme in a pan and heat gently until the sugar has dissolved. Bring to the boil, then simmer for 3 minutes. Add the honey and lemon juice. Cool.

Strain into a rigid freezerproof container, cover, seal and freeze for 2 to 3 hours, until half frozen.

Whisk the egg white until stiff, then whisk into the ice. Spoon the sorbet into the lemon shells, piling it up well. Place upright on a tray and freeze for 2 hours, until solid. Freeze any remaining sorbet in a rigid container, for another occasion.

Transfer to the refrigerator 10 minutes before serving to soften. Decorate with thyme sprigs.

Serves 4

Raspberry Yogurt Sorbet

250 g (8 oz) raspberries
2 × 150 g (5.2 oz) cartons natural yogurt
1 tablespoon gelatine, soaked in 3 tablespoons cold water
2 egg whites
75 g (3 oz) caster sugar

Work the raspberries in an electric blender or food processor until smooth, then sieve to remove pips. Stir in the yogurt.

Heat the gelatine gently until dissolved then add to the purée.

Whisk the egg whites until stiff, then gradually whisk in the sugar. Carefully fold the purée into the meringue, turn into a rigid freezerproof container, cover, seal and freeze until firm.

Transfer to the refrigerator 30 minutes before serving to soften. Scoop into chilled glasses to serve.

Serves 6

Redcurrant Sherbet

500 g (1 lb) redcurrants
125 g (4 oz) icing sugar, sifted
juice of 1 orange
1 egg white
TO DECORATE:
frosted currant leaves (see below)
few sprigs redcurrants

Place the redcurrants, icing sugar and orange juice in an electric blender or food processor and work to a purée. Sieve to remove the pips. Place in a rigid freezerproof container, cover, seal and freeze for 2 to 3 hours. Whisk to break up the crystals.

Whisk the egg white until stiff, then whisk into the half-frozen purée. Return to the freezer until firm. Transfer to the refrigerator 15 minutes before serving to soften.

Scoop into chilled glasses and decorate with frosted currant leaves and redcurrant sprigs.

Serves 4

Frosted Leaves: Paint egg white all over the leaves with a fine paintbrush. Brush off any excess and dip in caster sugar until completely coated. Place on greaseproof paper to dry for 1 to 2 hours.

Coffee Granita

75 g (3 oz) soft brown sugar
600 ml (1 pint) water
2 tablespoons coffee granules
TOPPING:
2 tablespoons Tia Maria
120 ml (4 fl oz) whipping cream, whipped
1 teaspoon coffee granules

Place the sugar and water in a heavy-based pan and heat gently until dissolved. Bring to the boil; boil for 5 minutes, add the coffee; cool.

Pour into a rigid freezerproof container, cover, seal and freeze for 2 hours. Whisk and return to the freezer for 2 hours. Whisk again and return to the freezer until firm.

Leave at room temperature for 10 minutes, then stir until crumbly. Spoon into tall glasses. Pour a little liqueur over each, top with a whirl of cream, and sprinkle with coffee.

Serves 4 to 6

Lemon Granita

125 g (4 oz) caster sugar
600 ml (1 pint) water
thinly pared rind and juice of 3 lemons
4 lemon twists to decorate

Gently heat the sugar and water in a pan with the lemon rind until dissolved, then boil for 5 minutes. Add the lemon juice, cool, then strain.

Freeze and serve as for Coffee granita (above), replacing the topping with lemon twists.

Serves 4

Gooseberry Sorbet

500 g (1 lb) gooseberries
2 heads elderflower, tied in muslin (optional)
125 g (4 oz) sugar
150 ml (1/4 pint) water
1 egg white
elderflower or mint leaves to decorate

Put the gooseberries in a pan with the elderflower, if using, sugar and water. Cover and simmer for 15 minutes until tender. Remove the elderflower, cool slightly, then work in an electric blender or food processor until smooth. Sieve, then leave to cool.

Turn into a rigid freezerproof container, cover, seal and freeze for 2 to 3 hours, until slushy.

Whisk the egg white until stiff and fold into the purée. Freeze until firm.

Transfer to refrigerator 10 minutes before serving to soften. Scoop into chilled glasses and decorate with elderflower or mint leaves.

Serves 4

Iced Strawberry Ring

568 ml (1 pint) whipping cream
2 tablespoons brandy
1 tablespoon icing sugar, sifted
125 g (4 oz) meringues

TO FINISH:
142 ml (5 fl oz) double cream, whipped
350 g (12 oz) strawberries, halved

Place the cream, brandy and icing sugar in a bowl and whip until it stands in soft peaks. Break the meringues into pieces and fold into the cream.

Turn into a 1.5 litre (2½ pint) ring mould. Cover with foil, seal and freeze until firm.

Turn out onto a serving dish 30 minutes before serving and place in the refrigerator. Pipe cream around the edge and fill the centre with strawberries to serve.

Serves 8

Strawberry Ice Cream Soufflé

500 g (1 lb) strawberries
4 eggs, separated
175 g (6 oz) caster sugar
250 ml (8 fl oz) double cream, whipped

Tie a band of foil very tightly around a 900 ml (1½ pint) freezerproof soufflé dish to stand 5 cm (2 inches) above the rim.

Reserve 6 strawberries for decoration. Work the remainder in an electric blender or food processor to a purée. Sieve to remove pips.

Place the egg yolks and sugar in a bowl and whisk with an electric mixer until thick and creamy. Fold the purée into the cream, then fold into the egg mixture. Whisk the egg whites until stiff, then carefully fold into the strawberry mixture. Turn into the prepared dish and freeze until firm.

Transfer to the refrigerator 30 minutes before serving to soften. Remove the foil carefully. Decorate with strawberry slices.

Serves 8

Iced Zabaione

4 egg yolks
75 g (3 oz) icing sugar, sifted
4 tablespoons Marsala
120 ml (4 fl oz) double cream
chopped pistachio nuts or toasted almonds to decorate

Place the egg yolks in a bowl with the icing sugar and whisk with an electric mixer until thick and mousse-like. Whip the Marsala and cream together until thick, then carefully fold into the egg mixture.

Pour into 4 freezerproof ramekin dishes, cover, seal and freeze. Sprinkle with chopped nuts to serve.

Serves 4

Mango Ice Cream

2 ripe mangoes
284 ml (½ pint) single cream
125 g (4 oz) icing sugar, sifted
juice of 2 limes or small lemons

Cut the mangoes in half lengthways, scrape out the flesh and discard the stones. Place the flesh in an electric blender or food processor with the remaining ingredients and work to a purée. Pour into a rigid freezerproof container, cover, seal and freeze for 2 hours. Remove from the freezer, whisk well, then re-freeze until firm.

Transfer to the refrigerator 30 minutes before serving to soften. Scoop into chilled glasses to serve.

Serves 6 to 8

Gooseberry Ice Cream

500 g (1 lb) gooseberries
125 g (4 oz) caster sugar
2 tablespoons water
3 egg whites
75 g (3 oz) icing sugar, sifted
few drops of green food colouring
142 ml (5 fl oz) double cream, whipped
frosted mint leaves (see page 43) to decorate

Place the gooseberries in a pan with the sugar and water. Cover and cook gently for 10 to 15 minutes until tender. Purée in a blender or food processor, then sieve. Leave to cool.

Whisk the egg whites until stiff, then gradually whisk in the icing sugar. Fold in the purée, food colouring and cream.

Turn into a rigid freezerproof container, cover, seal and freeze.

Transfer to the refrigerator 30 minutes before serving to soften. Scoop into chilled glasses and decorate with frosted mint leaves.

Serves 6 to 8

Raspberry Bombe

250 g (8 oz) raspberries
3 tablespoons icing sugar
284 ml (½ pint) double cream
142 ml (5 fl oz) single cream
125 g (4 oz) meringues
raspberries to decorate (optional)

Place the raspberries and icing sugar in an electric blender or food processor and blend until smooth; sieve to remove the pips.

Whip the double and single creams together until they form soft peaks. Break the meringues into pieces and fold into the cream.

Very lightly fold half the raspberry purée into the cream mixture to give a marbled effect. Turn into a 1.2 litre (2 pint) pudding basin, cover with foil, seal and freeze until firm.

Turn out onto a serving plate and place in the refrigerator 40 minutes before serving to soften. Pour the remaining purée over the bombe to serve. Decorate with fresh raspberries if desired.

Serves 6

Apple and Blackcurrant Ice Cream

250 g (8 oz) cooking apples, peeled, cored and sliced
250 g (8 oz) blackcurrants
2 tablespoons granulated sugar
4 tablespoons water
4 eggs, separated
125 g (4 oz) caster sugar
284 ml (½ pint) double cream, whipped
frosted currant leaves to decorate (see page 43)

Place the apples in a large pan with the blackcurrants, granulated sugar and water. Cover and cook over a gentle heat until soft.

Cool slightly, then work in an electric blender or food processor to make a purée. Sieve to remove pips and leave to cool completely.

Whisk the egg whites until stiff, then gradually whisk in the caster sugar; whisk in the egg yolks. Fold the fruit purée into the cream, then fold into the egg mixture. Turn into a rigid freezerproof container, cover, seal and freeze until firm.

Transfer to the refrigerator 30 minutes before serving to soften.

Scoop into chilled glasses and decorate with frosted currant leaves.

Serves 8 to 10

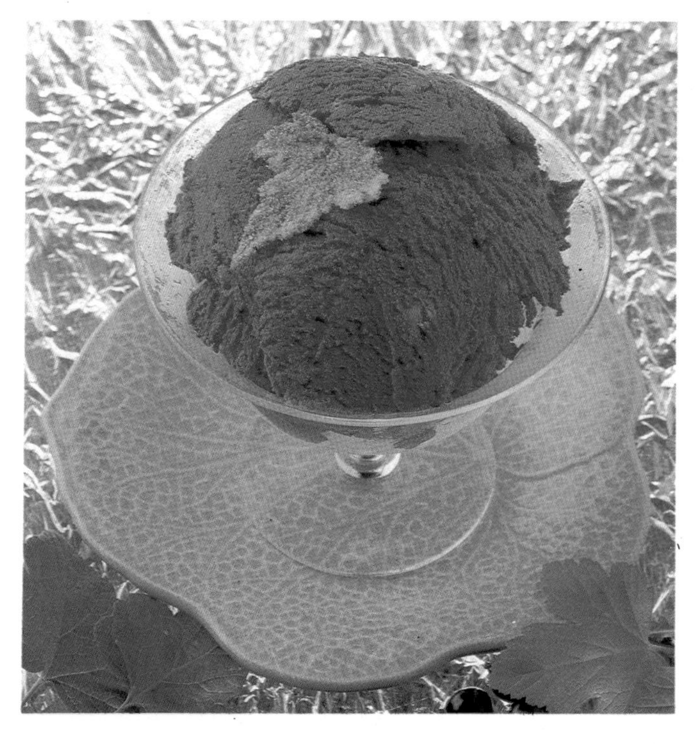

Mocha Bombe

250 g (8 oz) plain chocolate, chopped
COFFEE ICE CREAM:
2 tablespoons instant coffee powder
2 tablespoons boiling water
2 egg whites
125 g (4 oz) caster sugar
284 ml (½ pint) double cream

Melt the chocolate in a heatproof bowl over a pan of simmering water.

Put a 1.2 litre (2 pint) basin in the freezer to chill for 10 minutes. Pour the chocolate into the basin and rotate to coat the inside completely. Place the basin in a bowl of crushed ice and continue rotating until the chocolate has set in a layer.

To make the ice cream, mix the coffee with the water; leave to cool. Whisk the egg whites until stiff, then gradually whisk in the sugar. Whip the cream with the coffee mixture until it forms soft peaks. Fold into the meringue mixture.

Spoon into the chocolate mould, smooth the top evenly, cover with foil and freeze until firm.

Dip the basin into cold water, invert onto a serving plate and give a sharp shake to turn out.

Serves 6 to 8

Truffle and Coffee Ripple

TRUFFLE MIXTURE:
125 g (4 oz) plain chocolate, chopped
2 tablespoons single cream
2 tablespoons rum

COFFEE ICE CREAM:
2 tablespoons instant coffee powder
2 tablespoons boiling water
2 egg whites
125 g (4 oz) caster sugar
284 ml (½ pint) double cream

Put the truffle ingredients in a heat-proof bowl over a pan of simmering water until the chocolate has melted. Mix well, then leave to cool.

Meanwhile, make the ice cream: dissolve the coffee in the water and leave to cool. Whisk the egg whites until stiff, then gradually whisk in the sugar. Whip the cream with the coffee until it forms soft peaks. Fold into the meringue mixture.

When the truffle mixture begins to thicken, stir until smooth and soft. Fold into the ice cream mixture, very lightly to create a marbled effect. Turn into a rigid freezerproof container, cover, seal and freeze until firm.

Transfer to the refrigerator 15 minutes before serving, to soften. Scoop into chilled glasses and serve with Chocolate Sauce (see page 92) if desired.

Serves 8

Pineapple Parfait

1 large pineapple
125 g (4 oz) caster sugar
2 egg whites
284 ml (½ pint) double cream, whipped
2 tablespoons kirsch

Cut the pineapple in half lengthways. Scrape out the flesh and juice into an electric blender or food processor. Add 1 tablespoon of the sugar and work to a purée.

Transfer to a rigid freezerproof container, cover, seal and freeze for 1 to 2 hours, until half frozen.

Whisk the egg whites until stiff, then whisk in the remaining sugar, a tablespoon at a time. Whisk the half frozen purée, then fold into the meringue mixture with the cream and kirsch.

Spoon into chilled glasses and serve immediately, with Tuiles d'Oranges (see page 90).

Serves 6 to 8

Pina Colada Ice

1 large pineapple
25 g (1 oz) creamed coconut, chopped
2 tablespoons boiling water
2 egg whites
125 g (4 oz) caster sugar
6 tablespoons white rum
284 ml (½ pint) whipping cream, whipped

Cut the pineapple in half lengthways. Scrape out the flesh and juice into a bowl, discarding the hard core. Chill the shells in the refrigerator. Work the flesh and juice in an electric blender or food processor to make a purée.

Blend the coconut cream with the boiling water; leave to cool.

Whisk the egg whites until stiff, then gradually whisk in the sugar.

Mix the pineapple purée with the coconut and rum. Fold this into the cream with the meringue mixture. Turn into a rigid freezerproof container, cover, seal and freeze for 1½ hours. Remove from the freezer and stir well, then re-freeze until firm.

Transfer to the refrigerator 30 minutes before serving to soften. Scoop into the chilled pineapple shells and arrange on a dish.

Serves 8 to 10

Ginger Ice Cream

120 ml (4 fl oz) water
75 g (3 oz) granulated sugar
3 egg yolks
284 ml (½ pint) double cream
75 g (3 oz) preserved stem ginger, finely chopped

Place the water and sugar in a pan and heat gently, stirring until dissolved. Increase the heat and boil steadily until the syrup reaches a temperature of 110°C (225°F); at this stage a little of the cooled syrup will form a thread when drawn between the thumb and forefinger.

Cool slightly, then pour onto the egg yolks, whisking until the mixture is thick and mousse-like.

Whip the cream until it stands in soft peaks, then fold in the ginger. Fold into the egg mixture. Turn into a rigid freezerproof container. Cover, seal and freeze until firm.

Transfer to the refrigerator 20 minutes before serving to soften. Scoop into chilled glasses to serve.

Serves 4 to 6

Rum and Raisin Ice Cream

75 g (3 oz) seedless raisins
4 tablespoons dark rum
3 egg yolks
125 g (4 oz) soft brown sugar
284 ml (½ pint) single cream
284 ml (½ pint) double cream, whipped

Place the raisins and rum in a bowl and leave to soak.

Place the egg yolks and sugar in a heatproof bowl and whisk, using an electric mixer, until thick and mousse-like. Bring the single cream to just below boiling point and stir into the egg mixture. Place the bowl over a pan of simmering water and stir until thickened. Strain and cool.

Fold the double cream into the cooled custard mixture. Transfer to a rigid freezerproof container, cover, seal and freeze for 2 to 3 hours, until there is 2.5 cm (1 inch) of solid ice cream around the sides.

Mix well until smooth, then stir in the rum and raisins. Return to the freezer until firm.

Transfer to the refrigerator 20 minutes before serving to soften. Scoop into chilled glasses to serve.

Serves 8

Maple and Walnut Ice Cream

450 ml ($^3/_4$ pint) double cream
142 ml (5 fl oz) single cream
25 g (1 oz) soft brown sugar
6 tablespoons maple syrup
4 tablespoons dark rum
75 g (3 oz) walnut pieces, chopped

Place the creams, sugar, syrup and rum in a bowl and whip until it holds its shape. Fold in the nuts. Turn into a rigid freezerproof container, cover, seal and freeze until firm.

Transfer to the refrigerator 30 minutes before serving to soften. Scoop into chilled glass dishes. Serve with Fudge Sauce (see page 92), or extra maple syrup, and Langues de Chat biscuits (see page 87).
Serves 6

Orange Ice Cream

4 large oranges
4 egg yolks
125 g (4 oz) caster sugar
284 ml (½ pint) single cream
142 ml (¼ pint) double cream, whipped
6-8 chocolate triangles (see page 73) to decorate

Halve two of the oranges, carefully scoop out the flesh and juice and sieve to extract all juices; keep on one side. Freeze the orange shells.

Finely grate the rind of the remaining oranges and place in a heat-proof bowl with the egg yolks and sugar. Beat until thoroughly blended. Heat the single cream to just below boiling point; stir into the egg yolk mixture. Place the bowl over a pan of simmering water and stir until thickened. Add the orange juice, strain and cool.

Fold the orange custard into the double cream and turn into a rigid freezerproof container. Cover, seal and freeze until firm.

Scoop into the reserved orange shells, piling up well. Return the leftover ice cream to the freezer for another occasion or scoop into extra shells.

Decorate each with a chocolate triangle and serve immediately, or return to the freezer until required.

Serves 6 to 8

Chocolate and Orange Slice

ORANGE ICE CREAM:
finely grated rind and juice of 2 oranges
3 eggs, separated
150 g (5 oz) caster sugar
284 ml (½ pint) double cream, lightly whipped

CHOCOLATE LAYER:
125 g (4 oz) plain chocolate, chopped
4 tablespoons single cream

TO FINISH:
142 ml (5 fl oz) double cream, whipped
chocolate rose leaves (see page 78)

Put the orange rind, egg yolks and half the sugar in a bowl. Whisk with an electric mixer until thick. Whisk the egg whites until stiff; gradually whisk in the remaining sugar.

Whisk the orange juice into the whipped cream. Fold into the egg mixture, then fold into the meringue mixture. Turn into a rigid freezerproof container, cover, seal and freeze until firm.

Place the chocolate and cream in a small pan and heat gently until the chocolate has melted; cool.

Spread half the ice cream in a 1 kg (2 lb) loaf tin evenly. Spread the chocolate mixture smoothly over the top and freeze for 20 minutes. Return remaining ice cream to the freezer.

When the chocolate layer has set, carefully spread the remaining ice cream on top and smooth. Cover with foil, seal and freeze until firm.

Turn out onto a serving plate, decorate with piped cream and finish with rose leaves.

Serves 8

Chocolate and Orange Ice Cream

2 egg yolks
50 g (2 oz) caster sugar
grated rind and juice of 1 orange
175 g (6 oz) plain chocolate, chopped
284 ml (½ pint) single cream
284 ml (½ pint) double cream, whipped
finely shredded orange rind, to decorate

Beat the egg yolks, sugar and orange rind together. Put the chocolate and single cream in a heatproof bowl over a pan of simmering water until melted. Pour onto the egg mixture, stirring vigorously, then return to the bowl and heat gently until thickened. Add the orange juice and leave to cool.

Fold in three quarters of the double cream and turn into a 900 ml (1½ pint) loaf tin. Cover with foil, seal and freeze until firm.

Turn out onto a plate 30 minutes before serving. Decorate with the remaining cream and orange rind and allow to soften in the refrigerator.

Serves 6

Chocolate Bombe Noel

125 g (4 oz) glacé cherries, chopped
125 g (4 oz) raisins
50 g (2 oz) angelica, chopped
50 g (2 oz) crystallized pineapple (optional)
50 g (2 oz) sultanas
6 tablespoons rum
3 egg yolks
75 g (3 oz) caster sugar
175 g (6 oz) plain chocolate, chopped
284 ml (½ pint) single cream
284 ml (½ pint) double cream, whipped
125 g (4 oz) blanched almonds, chopped and toasted

Place the fruit in a bowl, stir in the rum and leave to soak for 1 hour.

Beat the egg yolks and sugar in a heatproof bowl, using an electric whisk, until thick and mousse-like. Gently melt the chocolate in a pan with the single cream, then heat to just below boiling point. Beat into the egg yolk mixture. Place over a pan of simmering water and stir until thickened. Strain and cool.

Fold the custard into half the double cream. Pour into a rigid freezerproof container, cover, seal and freeze for 2 hours. Remove from the freezer.

Stir well and mix in the fruit, rum and almonds. Turn into a 1.75 litre (3 pint) pudding basin, cover with foil, seal and freeze until firm.

Dip the basin into cold water and turn out onto a chilled plate. Smooth the surface and decorate with the remaining cream and a sprig of holly.

Serves 6 to 8

Iced Chocolate Soufflés

4 eggs, separated
125 g (4 oz) icing sugar, sifted
75 g (3 oz) plain chocolate, chopped
1 tablespoon water
250 ml (8 fl oz) double cream
2 tablespoons rum
grated chocolate to decorate

Tie a double band of foil very tightly around 6 freezerproof ramekin dishes to stand 2.5 cm (1 inch) above the rim.

Place the egg yolks and icing sugar in a bowl and whisk with an electric mixer until thick and creamy.

Place the chocolate and water in a small pan and heat very gently until melted. Cool slightly, then whisk into the egg mixture.

Whip the cream with the rum until it stands in soft peaks, then fold in the chocolate mixture.

Whisk the egg whites until stiff and carefully fold into the mousse. Pour into the prepared ramekins and freeze for 4 hours until firm.

Transfer to the refrigerator 10 minutes before serving to soften. Remove the foil carefully. Sprinkle the chocolate over the top to cover completely.

Serves 4 to 6

Chocolate Mint Ice

2 egg whites
125 g (4 oz) caster sugar
1 × 410 g (14.5 oz) can evaporated milk, chilled
4 drops of green food colouring
½ teaspoon peppermint essence
75 g (3 oz) plain chocolate, finely chopped

Whisk the egg whites until stiff, then gradually whisk in the sugar. Place the evaporated milk in a bowl with the colouring and peppermint essence. Whisk until thick, then fold into the meringue mixture with the chocolate.

Turn into a rigid freezerproof container, cover, seal and freeze for 2 hours.

Remove from the freezer and stir vigorously. Re-freeze until firm.

Transfer to the refrigerator 1 hour before serving to soften. Scoop into chilled glass dishes and serve with Cigarettes Russes (see page 88).

Serves 8

Chocolate Cups

284 ml (1/2 pint) single cream
250 g (8 oz) plain chocolate, chopped
4 egg yolks
3 tablespoons brandy
chocolate curls to decorate (see below)

Place the cream in a pan and heat just to boiling point. Pour into a blender or food processor and add the chocolate. Blend on maximum speed for 30 seconds. Add the egg yolks and brandy and blend for 10 seconds. Pour into glasses or small cups and chill until required. Sprinkle with chocolate curls to serve.

Serves 8

Chocolate Curls: Shave thin layers from a block of chocolate with a potato peeler.

Chocolate and Orange Mousse

125 g (4 oz) plain chocolate, broken into pieces
grated rind and juice of 1 small orange
3 eggs, separated
3 tablespoons double cream, whipped
finely shredded orange rind to decorate

Place the chocolate in a heatproof bowl with the orange rind and juice. Place over a pan of simmering water until melted. Mix in the egg yolks.

Whisk the egg whites until fairly stiff, then fold into the chocolate mixture. Pour into individual glasses and chill until set.

Pipe a rosette of cream on each mousse and decorate with orange rind.

Serves 4 to 6

Coffee and Brandy Soufflé

3 eggs, separated
75 g (3 oz) caster sugar
300 ml (½ pint) milk
2 tablespoons instant coffee granules
15 g (½ oz) gelatine, soaked in 3 tablespoons cold water
284 ml (½ pint) double cream
3 tablespoons brandy
2 tablespoons finely chopped almonds, browned

Tie a band of double greaseproof paper around a 1 litre (1¾ pint) soufflé dish to stand 5 cm (2 inches) above the rim; oil the inside of the paper.

Place the egg yolks and sugar in a bowl and beat until creamy. Place the milk in a pan with the coffee and bring to the boil. Pour onto the egg yolk mixture, stirring well. Return to the pan and cook gently, stirring constantly, until the custard coats the back of a spoon. Remove from the heat, add the gelatine and stir until dissolved. Leave to cool, stirring occasionally.

Place the cream in a bowl with the brandy and whip until stiff. Reserve a quarter for decoration.

When the custard is beginning to set, fold into the cream. Whisk the egg whites until stiff and stir 2 tablespoons into the coffee mixture to soften it. Carefully fold in the remaining egg white and turn into the prepared dish. Leave to set in the refrigerator.

Remove the paper carefully and press the almonds around the side. Decorate with piped cream.

Serves 6 to 8

Coffee and Walnut Cream

12 marshmallows
120 ml (4 fl oz) strong black coffee
284 ml (½ pint) double cream
50 g (2 oz) walnut pieces, chopped

Place the marshmallows in a pan with the coffee and heat gently, stirring until dissolved. Allow to cool.

Whip the cream until it stands in soft peaks, then carefully fold into the coffee mixture with all but 2 teaspoons of the walnuts.

Spoon into individual dishes and sprinkle with the remaining walnuts. Serve chilled.

Serves 4

Chocolate Brandy Gâteau

350 g (12 oz) plain chocolate, broken into pieces
4 tablespoons strong black coffee
4 tablespoons brandy
250 g (8 oz) digestive biscuits, broken into small pieces
175 g (6 oz) glacé cherries, quartered
TO FINISH:
250 ml (8 fl oz) double cream, whipped
chocolate caraque, made with 50 g (2 oz) chocolate (see below)

Place the chocolate and coffee in a pan and heat gently until melted; do not allow to become more than lukewarm. Remove from the heat and add the brandy, biscuits and cherries. Mix thoroughly, then turn into a greased 18 cm (7 inch) loose-bottomed cake tin. Smooth the top and chill overnight in the refrigerator.

Remove from the tin and slide onto a plate. Pipe the cream over the top of the gâteau. Decorate with chocolate caraque.

Serves 8

Chocolate Caraque: Spread a thin layer of melted chocolate onto a marble slab. Leave until firm, but not hard. Draw a sharp, thin-bladed knife at a slight angle across the chocolate with a slight sawing movement, scraping off thin layers to form long scrolls.

Chocolate Hazelnut Meringue

MERINGUE:
4 egg whites
250 g (8 oz) caster sugar
125 g (4 oz) hazelnuts, toasted and ground

FILLING:
125 g (4 oz) plain chocolate, broken into pieces
4 tablespoons water
450 ml (¾ pint) double cream

TO FINISH:
50 g (2 oz) chocolate, melted

Whisk the egg whites until stiff then whisk in 2 tablespoons of the sugar. Carefully fold in the remaining sugar a little at a time, with the ground hazelnuts.

Put the meringue into a piping bag fitted with a 1 cm (½ inch) plain nozzle and pipe into two 23 cm (9 inch) rounds on baking sheets lined with silicone paper. Bake in a preheated very cool oven, 120°C (250°F), Gas Mark ½, for 2 hours. Transfer to a wire rack to cool.

Place the chocolate and water in a small pan and heat very gently until melted; cool. Whip the cream until it begins to thicken, then whip in the cooled chocolate and continue to whip until stiff.

Use three quarters of the chocolate cream to sandwich the meringue rounds together. Pipe the remaining cream around the top edge. Put the melted chocolate in a greaseproof piping bag, snip off the end and drizzle the chocolate across the top of the meringue.

Serves 8

Chocolate Cherry Shortcake

125 g (4 oz) butter
50 g (2 oz) caster sugar
150 g (5 oz) plain flour, sifted
25 g (1 oz) cocoa, sifted
284 ml (½ pint) double cream, whipped
350 g (12 oz) fresh or canned black cherries, stoned
sifted icing sugar for sprinkling

Cream the butter and sugar together until soft and creamy, then stir in the flour and cocoa. Mix to a firm dough, turn onto a floured surface and knead lightly. Divide the mixture in half and roll each piece into a 20 cm (8 inch) round on a baking sheet.

Bake in a preheated moderate oven, 180°C (350°F), Gas Mark 4, for 20 minutes. Leave for 2 minutes, then cut one round into 8 sections. Carefully slide both rounds onto a wire rack to cool.

Reserve 2 tablespoons of the cream. Mix the rest with the cherries and spread over the chocolate round.

Arrange the cut sections on top and sprinkle with icing sugar. Decorate with the reserved cream.

Serves 8

Mocha Hazelnut Torte

75 g (3 oz) plain chocolate
3 tablespoons water
50 g (2 oz) butter
50 g (2 oz) soft light brown sugar
1 egg yolk
50 g (2 oz) hazelnuts, toasted and ground
2 tablespoons dark rum
4 tablespoons strong black coffee
16 sponge fingers
284 ml (½ pint) double cream, whipped
hazelnuts to decorate

Place the chocolate and water in a small pan and heat gently until melted; leave to cool.

Cream the butter and sugar together until light and fluffy. Add the egg yolk and beat thoroughly. Beat in the cooled chocolate and ground hazelnuts.

Mix the rum and coffee together; dip in the sponge fingers, and use half to cover the base of a lined and greased 500 g (1 lb) loaf tin.

Spread a quarter of the cream on top, then cover with the chocolate mixture. Spread one third of the remaining cream on top and cover with the remaining sponge fingers. Chill in the refrigerator until set.

Turn out onto a serving plate, pipe the remaining cream on top and decorate with hazelnuts.

Serves 6 to 8

Tartufi

125 g (4 oz) plain chocolate, chopped
2 teaspoons instant coffee powder
2 tablespoons water
2 tablespoons dark rum
284 ml (½ pint) double cream
75 g (3 oz) blanched almonds, chopped and toasted
6 chocolate rose leaves to decorate (see page 78)

Place the chocolate and coffee in a pan with the water. Heat very gently until melted. Add the rum and leave to cool.

Whip the cream until thick and fold in the chocolate mixture and almonds. Spoon into individual dishes and decorate with chocolate rose leaves. Serve chilled.

Serves 6

Chocolate Chestnut Charlotte

125 g (4 oz) plain chocolate, chopped
300 ml (½ pint) milk
2 eggs, separated
50 g (2 oz) soft light brown sugar
15 g (½ oz) gelatine, soaked in 3 tablespoons cold water
½ × 439 g (15½ oz) can unsweetened chestnut purée
284 ml (½ pint) double cream, whipped
30 Langues de Chat biscuits (see page 87)
chocolate triangles (see below)

Gently heat the chocolate in a small pan with the milk until melted.

Beat the egg yolks and sugar together until creamy, then stir in the chocolate mixture. Return to the pan and heat gently, stirring until thickened. Stir in the gelatine.

Beat the chestnut purée with a little of the custard until smooth, then mix in the remainder. Cool, then fold in two thirds of the cream. Whisk the egg whites until stiff and fold in. Turn into a lightly oiled deep 18 cm (7 inch) cake tin and chill until set.

Turn out onto a plate and cover with a thin layer of cream. Press the biscuits around the side; trim to fit if necessary. Decorate with remaining cream and chocolate triangles.

Serves 8

Chocolate Triangles: Melt 40 g (1½ oz) chocolate and spread thinly on a piece of greaseproof paper. When set, but not hard, cut into triangles, using a sharp knife and ruler.

Chocolate Orange Cheesecake

50 g (2 oz) butter
125 g (4 oz) digestive biscuits, finely crushed
25 g (1 oz) demerara sugar
454 g (1 lb) curd cheese
50 g (2 oz) caster sugar
grated rind and juice of 2 oranges
250 ml (8 fl oz) single cream
15 g (½ oz) gelatine, soaked in 3 tablespoons cold water
50 g (2 oz) plain chocolate, melted
TO DECORATE:
120 ml (4 fl oz) double cream, whipped

Melt the butter in a pan and stir in the biscuit crumbs and sugar. Spread the mixture over the base of a greased 20 cm (8 inch) loose-bottomed cake tin and press down. Leave in the refrigerator until firm.

Place the cheese in a bowl with the sugar and orange rind and beat until smooth. Strain the orange juice and add to the mixture, then gradually stir in the cream.

Heat the gelatine gently until dissolved, then stir into the cheese mixture. Pour over the crumb base. Pour the cooled, melted chocolate over the top, swirling with a fork to give a marbled effect. Chill in the refrigerator until set.

Remove from the tin and place on a serving plate. Pipe the cream around the edge to serve.

Serves 8

Hazelnut and Whisky Whip

50 g (2 oz) hazelnuts, skinned and finely chopped
50 g (2 oz) demerara sugar
50 g (2 oz) wholemeal breadcrumbs
284 ml (½ pint) double cream
150 g (5.2 oz) natural yogurt
3 tablespoons whisky
1 tablespoon clear honey

Combine the hazelnuts, sugar and breadcrumbs and place on a baking sheet. Put under a preheated hot grill until golden brown, stirring frequently. Leave to cool.

Whip the cream until it stands in soft peaks then whip in the yogurt, whisky and honey.

Fold in the hazelnut mixture, spoon into individual dishes and chill before serving.

Serves 6 to 8

Almond Crème Brulée

4 egg yolks
1 tablespoon caster sugar
568 ml (1 pint) double cream
few drops of vanilla essence
TO FINISH:
4 tablespoons chopped almonds
3 tablespoons soft brown sugar

Beat the egg yolks and sugar together. Warm the cream in a double saucepan or heatproof bowl over a pan of simmering water. Pour onto the egg mixture and stir well. Return to the pan or bowl and heat gently, stirring constantly, until thick enough to coat the back of a spoon. Add the vanilla essence.

Strain into 6 ramekin dishes and place in a roasting pan containing 2.5 cm (1 inch) water. Cook in a preheated cool oven, 140°C (275°F), Gas Mark 1, for 30 to 40 minutes.

Remove the ramekins, cool, then chill in the refrigerator overnight. Mix the almonds with the sugar and sprinkle over the custards to cover completely. Place under a preheated hot grill until the sugar caramelizes. Cool, then chill in the refrigerator for 1 hour before serving.

Serves 6

Chestnut Roulade

3 eggs, separated
125 g (4 oz) caster sugar
½ × 439 g (15½ oz) can unsweetened chestnut purée
grated rind and juice of 1 orange
sifted icing sugar for sprinkling
284 ml (½ pint) double cream
2 tablespoons Grand Marnier
finely shredded orange rind to decorate

Whisk the egg yolks with the sugar until thick and creamy. Put the chestnut purée in a bowl with the orange juice and beat until blended, then whisk into the egg mixture. Whisk the egg whites until fairly stiff and fold in carefully.

Turn into a lined and greased 20 × 30 cm (8 × 12 inch) Swiss roll tin. Bake in a preheated moderate oven, 180°C (350°F), Gas Mark 4, for 25 to 30 minutes, until firm.

Cool for 5 minutes, then cover with a clean damp cloth and leave until cold. Carefully turn the roulade onto a sheet of greaseproof paper, sprinkled thickly with icing sugar. Peel off the lining paper.

Place the cream, orange rind and liqueur in a bowl and whip until stiff. Spread three-quarters over the roulade and roll up like a Swiss roll. Transfer to a serving dish, pipe the remaining cream along the top and decorate with orange rind.

Serves 8

Nutty Profiteroles with Butterscotch Sauce

CHOUX PASTRY:
50 g (2 oz) butter
150 ml (¼ pint) water
65 g (2½ oz) plain flour, sifted
2 eggs, beaten
50 g (2 oz) blanched almonds, chopped
FILLING:
175 ml (6 fl oz) double cream
2 tablespoons Tia Maria
Butterscotch Sauce *(see page 92)*

Melt the butter in a large pan, add the water and bring to the boil. Add the flour all at once and beat until the mixture leaves the side of the pan. Cool slightly, then add the eggs a little at a time, beating vigorously.

Put the mixture into a piping bag fitted with a plain 1 cm (½ inch) nozzle and pipe small mounds on a dampened baking sheet. Sprinkle with the almonds.

Bake in a preheated hot oven, 220°C (425°F), Gas Mark 7, for 10 minutes, then lower the heat to 190°C (375°F), Gas Mark 5, and bake for a further 20 to 25 minutes, until golden. Make a slit in the side of each bun and cool on a wire rack.

Whip the cream with the liqueur until stiff. Spoon a little into each bun. Pile the profiteroles on a serving dish and pour over the warm butterscotch sauce to serve.

Serves 4 to 6

Chestnut Meringue Nests

MERINGUE:
3 egg whites
250 g (8 oz) caster sugar
FILLING:
½ × 439 g (15½ oz) can sweetened chestnut purée
1 tablespoon caster sugar
2 tablespoons brandy
142 ml (5 fl oz) whipping cream, whipped
8 chocolate rose leaves to decorate (see below)

Whisk the egg whites until stiff, then gradually whisk in the caster sugar.

Line a baking sheet with silicone paper and draw eight 7.5 cm (3 inch) circles on the paper. Put the meringue into a piping bag fitted with a large fluted nozzle. Pipe a round to fill each circle, then pipe round the edge of each base to form a nest.

Bake in a preheated cool oven, 140°C (275°F), Gas Mark 1, for 1½ hours. Cool on a wire rack. Remove the paper. Beat the chestnut purée with the sugar and brandy until blended, then fold in the cream. Put into a piping bag fitted with a large fluted nozzle and pipe into the nests.

Decorate each nest with a chocolate rose leaf.

Serves 8

Chocolate Rose Leaves: Coat the underside of each leaf with melted chocolate, using a fine paint brush. Leave to set, chocolate side up, then carefully lift the tip of the leaf and peel away from the chocolate.

Chestnut Whip

1 × 439 g (15½ oz) can unsweetened chestnut purée
50 g (2 oz) soft brown sugar
4 tablespoons brandy
juice of 1 small orange
284 ml (½ pint) double cream, whipped
finely shredded orange rind to decorate

Place the chestnut purée and sugar in a bowl and beat until smooth. Mix in the brandy and orange juice, then fold in the cream.

Spoon into glass dishes and decorate with orange rind.

Serves 8

Praline and Peach Gâteau

3 eggs
150 g (5 oz) caster sugar
grated rind of 1 lemon
75 g (3 oz) plain flour, sifted

PRALINE:
50 g (2 oz) whole almonds
50 g (2 oz) caster sugar

TO FINISH:
284 ml (½ pint) double cream, whipped
4 tablespoons apricot jam
2 teaspoons water
2 peaches, stoned and sliced

Place the eggs, sugar and lemon rind in a bowl and whisk with an electric mixer until thick and mousse-like. Carefully fold in the flour, then turn into a lined, greased and floured deep 20 cm (8 inch) cake tin.

Bake in a preheated moderately hot oven, 190°C (375°F), Gas Mark 5, for 30 to 35 minutes, until the cake springs back when lightly pressed. Turn onto a wire rack to cool.

Make the praline as for Praline Charlotte (see page 82) and fold half into two thirds of the cream. Split the cake in half and sandwich together with the praline cream.

Heat the jam with the water, sieve, reheat and use three quarters to glaze the side of the cake. Press the remaining praline around the side.

Arrange the peaches, overlapping, in a circle on top, leaving a border around the edge. Reheat remaining glaze and brush over the peaches.

Pipe the remaining cream in a decorative border around the edge.

Serves 6

Pineapple Hazelnut Pavlova

4 egg whites
250 g (8 oz) caster sugar
1 tablespoon cornflour
2 teaspoons vinegar
125 g (4 oz) hazelnuts, ground and toasted

FILLING:
1 small pineapple, thinly sliced
3 tablespoons kirsch
284 ml (½ pint) double cream
3 kiwi fruit, sliced

Whisk the egg whites until stiff. Add the sugar a tablespoon at a time, whisking until the meringue is very stiff. Whisk in the cornflour and vinegar, then carefully fold in the hazelnuts.

Pile the meringue onto a baking sheet lined with silicone paper and spread into a 20 cm (8 inch) round; hollow out the centre slightly. Bake in a preheated cool oven, 150°C (300°F), Gas Mark 2, for 1 hour. Leave to cool, peel off the paper and place on a serving dish.

Meanwhile, place the pineapple slices in a shallow dish, sprinkle with the kirsch and leave for 1 hour.

Place the cream in a bowl and add the kirsch from the pineapple. Whip until stiff, then spoon onto the pavlova, spreading to the edges.

Arrange the kiwi fruit slices overlapping in a circle round the edge. Lay the pineapple slices overlapping inside and finish with kiwi fruit in the centre.

Serves 8

Praline Charlotte

PRALINE:
50 g (2 oz) whole almonds
50 g (2 oz) caster sugar
CHARLOTTE:
18 sponge fingers
3 egg yolks
3 tablespoons icing sugar, sifted
350 ml (12 fl oz) milk
15 g (½ oz) gelatine, soaked in 3 tablespoons cold water
284 ml (½ pint) whipping cream, whipped
TO FINISH:
4 tablespoons double cream, whipped

First make the praline. Heat the almonds and sugar in a pan gently until melted, then cook until nut brown. Turn onto an oiled baking sheet. When hard, crush with a rolling pin.

Trim one end off each sponge finger to the height of a 1.5 litre (2½ pint) charlotte mould. Fit them closely, rounded end down, around the side of the lightly oiled mould.

Beat the egg yolks and icing sugar together until creamy. Bring the milk to the boil, then stir into the egg mixture. Return to the pan and cook gently, stirring until thickened. Strain into a bowl, add the gelatine and stir until dissolved. Cool.

Add three quarters of the praline and stir over a bowl of iced water until the mixture starts to thicken. Fold in the cream, pour into the prepared mould and chill until set.

To serve, invert onto a plate and decorate with the cream and remaining praline.

Serves 6

Pashka

2 × 227 g (8 oz) packets creamy soft cheese
1 egg yolk
75 g (3 oz) caster sugar
grated rind and juice of 1 lemon
120 ml (4 fl oz) double cream, whipped
50 g (2 oz) blanched almonds, chopped and browned
50 g (2 oz) glacé cherries, quartered
50 g (2 oz) raisins
25 g (1 oz) flaked almonds, toasted, to decorate

Place the cheese in a bowl with the egg yolk, sugar and lemon rind. Beat together thoroughly until smooth, then stir in the lemon juice. Fold in the cream with the chopped almonds and fruit.

Line a 1 litre (1¾ pint) clay flower pot or pudding basin with a piece of muslin large enough to overlap the top. Spoon in the cheese mixture and fold the cloth over. Cover with a saucer and place a 500 g (1 lb) weight on top. Place in a bowl and chill in the refrigerator overnight.

To serve, unfold the cloth, invert onto a serving plate and remove the muslin. Decorate with the almonds.
Serves 6 to 8

Petits Vacherins aux Noix

MERINGUE:
2 egg whites
125 g (4 oz) soft brown sugar
50 g (2 oz) walnuts, ground
FILLING:
2 tablespoons rum
142 ml (5 fl oz) double cream
TO DECORATE:
6 walnut halves

Whisk the egg whites until stiff, then whisk in the sugar, a tablespoon at a time. Carefully fold in the walnuts.

Line two baking sheets with silicone paper and draw six 7.5 cm (3 inch) circles and six 5 cm (2 inch) circles on the paper.

Put the meringue into a piping bag fitted with a 1 cm (½ inch) plain nozzle and pipe onto the circles to cover completely.

Bake in a preheated very cool oven, 120°C (250°F), Gas Mark ½, for 1½ to 2 hours. Transfer to a wire rack to cool.

Place the rum and cream in a bowl and whip until stiff. Put into a piping bag fitted with a large fluted nozzle and pipe three-quarters onto the larger circles. Cover with the small circles.

Decorate with the remaining cream and the walnut halves.

Serves 6

Apple and Walnut Whirls

75 g (3 oz) butter
50 g (2 oz) soft brown sugar
125 g (4 oz) plain flour, sifted
75 g (3 oz) walnuts, ground

FILLING:

1 tablespoon apricot jam
500 g (1 lb) dessert apples, peeled, cored and sliced
½ teaspoon ground cinnamon
250 ml (8 fl oz) double cream, whipped

TO DECORATE:

chopped walnuts

Cream the butter and sugar together until light and fluffy. Stir in the flour and walnuts, and mix to a firm dough, using your hand. Turn onto a floured surface and knead lightly until smooth. Roll the dough out thinly; cut out ten 7.5 cm (3 inch) and ten 5 cm (2 inch) circles. Place on a baking sheet and bake in a preheated moderate oven, 180°C (350°F), Gas Mark 4, for 12 to 15 minutes, until golden. Transfer to a wire rack to cool.

Place the jam and apples in a pan, cover and cook gently for 15 to 20 minutes, until softened, stirring occasionally. Add the cinnamon and leave to cool.

Spread the cooled apple mixture over the larger rounds, pipe two thirds of the cream over the apple and top with the small circles. Pipe the remaining cream on top and decorate with chopped walnuts.

Serves 10

Nutty Curls

75 g (3 oz) butter or margarine
75 g (3 oz) caster sugar
50 g (2 oz) plain flour
50 g (2 oz) hazelnuts, chopped

Cream the butter or margarine and sugar together until light and fluffy. Stir in the flour and hazelnuts and mix well. Place small teaspoonfuls of the mixture well apart on greased baking sheets and flatten with a damp fork.

Bake in a preheated moderately hot oven, 190° (375°F), Gas Mark 5, for 6 to 8 minutes, until pale golden.

Leave on the baking sheets for 1 minute, then remove with a palette knife and lay on rolling pins to curl. Leave until set then remove carefully.

Makes 25

Langues de Chats

50 g (2 oz) butter
50 g (2 oz) caster sugar
2 egg whites
50 g (2 oz) plain flour, sifted
few drops of vanilla essence

Cream the butter and sugar together until light and fluffy. Whisk the egg whites lightly and gradually beat into the creamed mixture with the flour and vanilla essence.

Place in a piping bag fitted with a 1 cm (3/8 inch) plain nozzle and pipe 7.5 cm (3 inch) lengths on greased and floured baking sheets; alternatively, pipe into rounds.

Bake in a preheated moderately hot oven, 200°C (400°F), Gas Mark 6, for 10 minutes; the biscuits should be pale golden, but darker around the edges. Transfer to a wire rack to cool.

Makes 20 to 24

Brandy Snaps

125 g (4 oz) butter
125 g (4 oz) demerara sugar
125 g (4 oz) golden syrup
125 g (4 oz) plain flour
1 teaspoon ground ginger

Put the butter, sugar and syrup in a saucepan and heat gently until the butter has melted and the sugar dissolved. Cool slightly, then sift in the flour and ginger. Beat well.

Place teaspoonfuls of the mixture 10 cm (4 inches) apart on baking sheets. Bake in a preheated moderate oven, 180°C (350°F), Gas Mark 4, for 10 to 12 minutes, until golden.

Leave to cool slightly, then remove with a palette knife and roll around the handle of a wooden spoon. Leave for 1 to 2 minutes to set, then slip off carefully onto a wire rack to cool.

Makes 35

NOTE: If the mixture cools and becomes too thick, spread it out thinly with a palette knife to flatten.

If the biscuits become too brittle to roll, return them to the oven for 30 seconds to soften.

Cigarettes Russes

1 egg white
50 g (2 oz) caster sugar
25 g (1 oz) butter, melted
15 g (½ oz) plain flour
¼ teaspoon vanilla essence

Place the egg white in a bowl. Add the sugar and beat until smooth. Add remaining ingredients and beat well.

Spread the mixture thinly into 10 × 6 cm (4 × 2½ inch) oblongs on greased and floured baking sheets. Bake in a preheated moderately hot oven, 200°C (400°F), Gas Mark 6, for 4 to 5 minutes, until golden.

Leave on the baking sheets for 30 seconds, then scrape off with a palette knife and place top side down on a table top. Roll each tightly around a small wooden spoon handle or pencil and hold firmly for a few seconds. Slide off and allow to cool.

Makes 15

NOTE: Do not bake more than 3 at a time or they will set before you have time to shape them.

Tuiles d'Oranges

1 egg white
50 g (2 oz) caster sugar
25 g (1 oz) plain flour
grated rind of ½ orange
25 g (1 oz) butter, melted

Place the egg white in a bowl and beat in the sugar. Add the remaining ingredients and mix well.

Place teaspoonfuls of the mixture well apart on greased baking sheets and spread out thinly with a palette knife.

Bake in a preheated moderately hot oven, 190°C (375°F), Gas Mark 5, for 6 to 8 minutes, until pale golden brown.

Leave on the baking sheets for a few seconds, then remove with a palette knife and place on a rolling pin to curl. Leave until cool then remove carefully.

Makes about 15

NOTE: Do not bake more than 4 at a time or they will set before you have time to shape them.

Lace Baskets

50 g (2 oz) butter or margarine
50 g (2 oz) demerara sugar
50 g (2 oz) golden syrup
50 g (2 oz) plain flour, sifted

Place the butter or margarine, sugar and syrup in a pan and heat gently until the fat has melted and the sugar dissolved. Cool slightly then beat in the flour.

Place 12 teaspoonfuls of the mixture at least 10 cm (4 inches) apart on 3 baking sheets. Bake in a preheated moderate oven, 180°C (350°F), Gas Mark 4, for 10 to 12 minutes, until golden.

Leave to cool slightly, then remove with a palette knife. Mould over the base of an inverted glass, with the top side of the biscuit touching the glass. Leave to set then remove carefully.

Makes 12

NOTE: If the mixture cools and becomes too thick, spread it out thinly with a palette knife to flatten.

Do not bake more than 4 at a time or they will set before you have time to mould them. If they become too brittle to handle, return them to the oven for 30 seconds to soften.

Chocolate Sauce

175 g (6 oz) plain chocolate, chopped
250 ml (8 fl oz) milk
1 teaspoon coffee granules
50 g (2 oz) soft brown sugar

Place all the ingredients in a small pan and heat gently until melted. Stir well and simmer, uncovered, for 2 to 3 minutes. Serve warm or cold, with vanilla, coffee or chocolate ice cream, or profiteroles.
Makes 450 ml (¾ pint)

Melba Sauce

350 g (12 oz) raspberries
50 g (2 oz) icing sugar, sifted

Place the raspberries and icing sugar in a blender or food processor. Blend to a purée, then sieve to remove the pips. Serve with vanilla ice cream.
Makes 150 ml (¼ pint)

Butterscotch Sauce

142 ml (5 fl oz) double cream
50 g (2 oz) unsalted butter
75 g (3 oz) soft dark brown sugar

Place the cream, butter and sugar in a pan. Heat gently, stirring, until the sugar has dissolved. Boil for 2 minutes until syrupy. Serve warm, with vanilla ice cream or profiteroles.
Makes 250 ml (8 fl oz)

Apricot Sauce

125 g (4 oz) dried apricots, soaked overnight in 600 ml (1 pint) water
50 g (2 oz) caster sugar
2 teaspoons lemon juice

Place the apricots and their soaking liquid in a pan, cover and simmer for 15 minutes. Add the sugar and lemon juice, stirring until the sugar has dissolved. Sieve or work in an electric blender or food processor until smooth. Serve hot or cold with vanilla ice cream.
Makes 450 ml (¾ pint)

Fudge Sauce

1 × 170 g (6 oz) can evaporated milk
50 g (2 oz) plain chocolate
50 g (2 oz) soft brown sugar

Place the ingredients in a small pan and heat gently, stirring, until the sugar has dissolved. Bring to the boil, then simmer for 2 to 3 minutes. Serve warm or cold, with vanilla, chocolate, coffee or maple and walnut ice cream.
Makes 250 ml (8 fl oz)

Mincemeat Sauce

2 dessert apples, peeled, cored and finely chopped
3 tablespoons water
250 g (8 oz) mincemeat
grated rind and juice of 1 orange
2 tablespoons brandy

Place the apples in a pan with the water. Cover and simmer gently for 5 minutes. Stir in the mincemeat, orange rind and juice and heat through. Stir in the brandy. Serve warm, with vanilla ice cream.
Makes 450 ml (¾ pint)

INDEX

Acknowledgments

Photography by Paul Williams
Food prepared by Carole Handslip
Photographic stylist: Penny Markham

The author should also like to thank ICTC
for the loan of equipment for recipe testing.